Published by Sweet Cherry Publishing Limited
Unit 36, Vulcan House,
Vulcan Road,
Leicester, LE5 3EF
United Kingdom

First published in the US in 2022
2022 edition

2 4 6 8 10 9 7 5 3 1

ISBN: 978-1-78226-502-3

© Harry Meredith

Soccer Rising Stars: Marcus Rashford

Cover design and illustrations
by Sophie Jones

Lexile® code numerical measure L = Lexile® 870L

www.sweetcherrypublishing.com

Printed and bound in Turkey

SOCCER RISING STARS

MARCUS RASHFORD

THE UNOFFICIAL STORY

Written by

HARRY MEREDITH

CONTENTS

1

MISSION IMPOSSIBLE

Rain poured onto the rooftop of the Parc des Princes in Paris. The stadium was filled with fans excited to watch their team play in a Champions League 16-16 tie. The home fans for Paris Saint Germain were confident, and they had reason to be:

they had come away with a 0-2 away victory in the first leg. The Manchester United fans, bunched together in the cold and miles away from home, knew that tonight was going to be difficult. They were coming up against the best team in France, while their own Premier League campaign had left much to be desired.

But this was the Champions League. And if there was a place for soccer miracles, this was it.

The teams emerged from the tunnel to the sound of the Champions League anthem. PSG were in their classic home uniform of navy blue and red, and Manchester United were wearing their pink 2017/2018 away uniform. The last player to appear from the tunnel was Marcus Rashford. Manchester United needed him to perform to the best of his ability if they were going to progress to the quarter-finals.

In the 2nd minute of the match, Rashford put pressure on the PSG defense as they passed the ball around at the back. This caused PSG defender Thilo Kehrer to play a loose pass toward his goalkeeper. Spotting his chance, the Manchester United forward Romelu

Lukaku claimed the ball and charged through on goal. He rounded the experienced Gianluigi Buffon and passed the ball into the net. *Goal!* The away fans roared. Manchester United had halved the deficit. Did they have a chance of coming back to win the tie?

In the 12th minute, PSG went on the attack. The ball was played to Kylian Mbappé in the penalty box and he thumped the ball across the six-yard line. Juan Bernat ran to the ball and  calmly slotted it into an open net. PSG had brought the game level and restored

10

their advantage. The French champions, undeterred by the earlier setback, were not going to give up their lead without a fight.

Less than twenty minutes later, the ball rebounded to Rashford in the opposition's half. He tapped the ball to the right, creating space, and unleashed a fearsome long-range strike. The ball swerved past the defenders and was on course for the bottom left corner. The goalkeeper managed to get in the way, but the strike was so powerful he could not catch it. Instead it stung his gloves and rebounded into the penalty area. The ball fell to the feet of Romelu Lukaku who passed the gift into an open net. *Yes!* There was still an hour of soccer left to play and all Manchester United needed was one more goal. Just one more moment of magic to shock everyone and knock PSG out of the competition.

The next major chance came in the second half—but it was for PSG. The ball was passed to the feet of Ángel Di María, a former Manchester United player. From inside the penalty box, he chipped the ball into the net. The home fans cheered and punched the air.

But their celebrations were abruptly halted. The linesman raised his flag. Di Maria was offside. Manchester United had gotten away with it, and they still needed just the one goal.

Chances fell to both sides in the remaining minutes, but no matter how hard they tried neither team could break through their opposition's defense. There were flying shots, diving saves, last-ditch tackles and amazing skills. But none of them led to the winning goal. The clock was close to striking ninety minutes and the game seemed to be over. Then Manchester United had one final chance.

Marcus sprinted with the ball toward the PSG goal, but there was no space for him. He looked to his right and saw Diogo Dalot charging toward the goal. Marcus' eyes followed his teammate's movement. With pinpoint accuracy he laid the ball off to Dalot, who shot at goal. The ball hit a PSG defender and bounced out for a corner. But as the ball hit the defender, Dalot raised his arms in the air.

"Handball!" he shouted. "Handball, ref!"

The other Manchester United players

raised their arms too. The referee hadn't seen the offence and pointed toward the corner flag. He was giving a corner kick to PSG. But as the team readied themselves to take it, VAR intervened. The referee was told that the ball might have hit a PSG defenders' arm. He went to look at the monitor. The shot was replayed over and over again, making sure that they checked every angle to make the correct decision.

The entire crowd fell silent: the PSG fans in fear; the Manchester United fans in hope. The referee turned from the monitor, brought his whistle to his mouth ... and pointed to the penalty spot! The PSG defender covered his face with his hands. The home fans booed, and the away fans cheered. Now Manchester United had a last-gasp chance to win the game.

As Manchester United's penalty taker, it was up to Marcus Rashford.

He placed the ball on the spot and walked to the edge of the box. The home fans jeered, trying to put him off. The goalkeeper swayed his arms and clapped his gloves together.

Marcus placed his hands on his hips, breathing slowly. The noise around him started to fade away. He visualized where he was going to put the ball and focused on one thing and one thing only. That was to score the winning goal and send his team—his boyhood team—through to the next round of the competition. The referee blew his whistle.

Marcus ran up to the ball and smashed it into the back of the net!

Goal! He sprinted into the corner, celebrating as loudly as his lungs would allow him. The Manchester United supporters cheered and hugged at the away end.

Marcus had done it. Now all they needed to do was hold on to the lead.

After a tense few minutes, the referee blew the whistle for the final time. The game was over. Marcus led the charge toward the celebrating away fans and the rest of the team sprinted with him across the field. A United fan through and through, Marcus reached the advertising boards and raised his fist in the air. Ten years earlier he would have been back home watching the goal on his TV. Tonight he was the one on the field. A Manchester United hero.

THE BOY FROM WYTHENSHAWE

Marcus Rashford was born on the 31st of October 1997. He was the fifth child in the family following Dwaine, Dane, Chantelle and Claire, all raised by his single mother, Melanie Maynard.

Melanie worked tirelessly for her family, working three jobs to earn

money. But she still struggled to put food on the table. It was not uncommon for Marcus to spend nights hungry—going to bed with a growling stomach and endless dreams of plates overflowing with food.

To make the most of free school meals, Marcus joined his elementary school's breakfast club. It meant that he had to get up early to go to school, but there was always a large bowl of cereal waiting for him. To Marcus, cereal was one of the best creations ever. He could not get enough of it. There were some days when he ate nothing but cereal. It was at breakfast club that Marcus met a lot of his school friends and children who had similar problems at home.

When Marcus' mind wasn't on food, there was another word beginning with "f" that he was focused on: soccer.

"Stop hogging it," said his brother Dwaine one day.

Marcus ran along the patch of grass outside his home, the ball stuck to his feet like glue. He sprinted in between his brothers and no matter how hard they tried, they just couldn't take the ball from him. He might have been the youngest in his family, but he was by far the most talented at soccer.

"Want to see how good my touch is?" said Marcus.

"Go on then, wonderboy," said Dane.

Marcus kicked the ball onto the roof of their home and it bounced back down. He controlled it perfectly as it fell.

"Bet you couldn't do it with your left," said Dwaine.

Marcus kicked the ball back onto the roof with his left foot, but this time as it hit, a tile cracked. It fell, seemingly in slow motion, before smashing into pieces on the ground. The three boys looked to one another with wide-eyed horror before bursting into laughter.

"Mom's gonna kill us," said Marcus.

"Us?" laughed Dwaine. "More like *you!*"

When not playing with his brothers, friends or any roof that he could bounce a ball off of, Marcus was playing soccer for Fletcher Moss Rangers. This was a local soccer team that was known for training talented soccer players from the area. Some famous players who also came from

the club were Wes Brown, Danny Welbeck and Jesse Lingard. Some kids went to develop their social skills and others went to simply play soccer. But it was historically one of the best clubs in the area for youngsters to join if they had hopes of making it as a professional.

Marcus thrived at Fletcher Moss Rangers. Some onlookers jokingly suggested that the team should start playing with two soccer balls—one for Marcus and another for the rest of the team. Without two, no one else would get a chance to play.

But it was when he played for the team in an under 7s local tournament that Marcus caught the eye of professional scouts. During one of the tournament matches, Marcus scored a mammoth twelve goals, showing everyone that he was the best player not only in that game, but in the entire tournament. He was recognized as such in a post-tournament awards ceremony, where he held the winning trophy with a winner's medal wrapped around his neck. After the tournament,

Marcus was given the opportunity to train with the Manchester City academy. As a Manchester United fan, this was a difficult decision to make. But he couldn't turn down the opportunity. A week later, after hearing that one of the most talented young players in the area was a fan, the Manchester United development team stepped in. They invited Marcus to come and train at the Manchester United academy instead.

Marcus didn't even need a second to contemplate his answer.

Yes!

For Manchester United, it was always going to be yes.

3

MANCHESTER UNITED ACADEMY

Marcus excelled at the academy. Scouts often thought that players around his age could be technically gifted. But when it came to being an athlete, that was often where players

fell short. This was never a concern for Marcus: he always had the energy, determination and desire to chase every opportunity. Whether that was when looking to make runs for a chance, or getting into space without the ball to demonstrate his soccer intelligence.

His abilities also proved useful in other sports. Marcus enjoyed playing cricket, tennis, pool and ping-pong. Yet none of them could ever match his love for soccer. During his first few years at the academy, Marcus showcased his talent and the coaches guided him in the right direction.

For boys between the ages of 12-16 at the academy, there was a scholarship program: the Manchester United Schoolboy Scholars (MANUSS) scheme. The most talented players from every age group were selected to train together. However, Marcus was only 11 years old – too young for the scheme. Yet with his struggles at home and his obvious talent, an

 exception was made for him to be considered for the scheme. Marcus' mother pushed for the academy to accept him on the scholarship a year early, to help ease the burden at home and to make sure he was given the best nutrition and development. After careful consideration it was decided that Marcus could join the scheme a year early. He was to move into academy housing, go to school at the club's partner academy and embrace a full-time program of soccer development.

"So it's this one?" asked Marcus, pointing at a house on a quiet road.

"Yeah, we're here," said his mom.

Marcus knocked with one hand, the

other lugging his heavy backpack.

A small lady, with a beaming and infectious smile, greeted them. "You must be Marcus," she said. "I'm Maria. Come in, come in."

Marcus followed his mom into the house and closed the door behind him. He rested the weight of the backpack against the door and looked around the room as the two adults talked. A muddy shoelace snuck out between the cracks of a cupboard door to his left. On top of the cupboard was a picture in a golden frame. Marcus thought that he recognized the figure, but couldn't quite make him out. He moved closer.

"You recognize my Gerry," Maria smiled.

"That's Gerard Piqué!" said Marcus. "Standing in front of this house!"

Maria laughed and picked up the photo, grinning as she examined it closely. "He used to live with me too," she said. "Hopefully you'll be just as successful as he was."

"He will be," said Marcus' mom, squeezing him tightly.

Marcus thought about Piqué and how he was now a professional soccer player. He played not only for a top club, but for his national team too. To be as successful as Piqué would be a dream come true! Marcus smiled. His nerves slowly turned into excitement.

"I'll leave you both to say goodbye," said Maria.

"Give me a hug, you." Marcus' mom wrapped her arms around him.

"I'll come see you all the time," said Marcus.

"You promise?" she said.

"Promise," said Marcus.

Marcus had to move away from everything he knew so that he could fully concentrate on soccer. He would be away from his family, his friends and his normal life. But it was a sacrifice he was willing to make. He was going to do everything he could to make it as a professional soccer player.

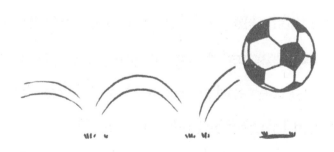

A LIFE-CHANGING THREE DAYS

Marcus' time at the academy flew by in a flash. He performed so well that he was fast-tracked from his age group, past the reserves and straight into the first team, not long after he had turned 18.

The Manchester United manager at the time, Louis Van Gaal, was so confident in Marcus' ability that he named him as a substitute for the second leg of a Europa League tie against Danish side FC Midtjylland. The Red Devils had played the first leg in Denmark and had returned with a shock 2-1 defeat. The team needed to put on a top performance in front of the home fans at Old Trafford in order to progress to the next round of the competition.

Marcus looked around the stadium in amazement at the tens of thousands of fans in attendance. He'd been named on the bench before, but had not yet made his debut for the club.

The coaches got the players to line up before taking some shooting drills. However, as Anthony Martial, the talented and leading forward for United, took his shot, he felt a pang of pain and fell to the ground. The medical team helped him into the locker room before checking his injury more closely. He'd damaged his hamstring and wouldn't be able to play. Still warming up on the field,

Marcus was focused and practicing with his teammates.

"Rashy!" shouted one of the coaches.

Marcus sprinted over.

"Tony's out." The coach explained. "He's done his hamstring. This is your chance, mate. Do us proud."

Marcus went into the locker room and was given a few words of advice by Van Gaal. Before he could take it all in, he was lining up in the Old

Trafford tunnel preparing to make his club debut. The fans hardly had any

39

idea about him. Some who kept up to date with the academy knew of his talents. But to most spectators he was unknown. It was up to Marcus to show the Manchester United faithful exactly what he could do.

In the 63rd minute of the second half, the ball was played into Juan Mata on the byline. He just about kept the ball in play and swung a cross into the box along the ground. Marcus burst through two defenders, his determination and hunger obvious to all. With his heart pounding, Marcus side-footed the ball into the back of the net. *Goal!* The crowd roared and Marcus ran straight to the corner of the stadium. Before the game he had been told that the academy players were seated there. He ran straight to his academy teammates and celebrated with them. Hugging, cheering and jumping. Not only had he made his senior debut for the club he adored, but he had also scored an important goal—and his first ever for the Manchester United first team.

Marcus did not stop there, though. Just over ten minutes later, Guillermo Varela crossed in the ball from the other side of the field and Marcus flew across the field hammering it into the net. He could hardly have dreamed of a better debut at the "theatre of dreams". He had scored two goals and helped his team fight back against the Danish side to progress to the next round of the tournament.

After the game Marcus was flooded with calls from friends and family. He had made himself and the whole of Manchester proud.

But Marcus' fairy-tale start to life in soccer wasn't fully written yet. Two days later, Manchester United had

a Premier League home tie against Arsenal – a rival and top side in the division. Delighted with Marcus' performance, the manager decided to play Marcus again. He was gifted his Premier League debut just tens of hours after his Europa League brace. He had only started in two U21 games and two professional soccer matches. His speedy progression to the first team was unheard of.

In the 29th minute of the Premier League fixture, Varela swung a cross ball into the Arsenal box. A defender got to the ball first but could only divert it rather than clear it. The ball perfectly fell to the ground and to the feet of the oncoming Marcus Rashford. He received it with thanks. Marcus smashed the ball into the net and sent the home fans wild. Marcus couldn't stop smiling as he ran to the fans and cheered. His teammates surrounded him, joining in with the celebrations.

Three minutes later, Marcus' performance turned into something from a dream. Another former Fletcher Moss Rangers player, Jesse Lingard, crossed the ball into the box

and Rashford leapt for
it. He headed the ball
into the net and scored
his second goal of the
game. The youngster, who

had hardly been known to united
fans a few days ago, was now known
to soccer fans everywhere. Not only
had he made his Premier and Europe
League debuts, but he had scored a
brace both times.

Marcus played for the majority of
the match and helped lead his team to
victory. He was brought off toward the
end of the game. Everyone knew that

they had just witnessed an incredible performance not just for Marcus, but for Manchester United. It was a proud moment in club history where one of their own had not only performed, but had absolutely excelled.

Marcus received a standing ovation from the stands and hugs, praise and high fives from the players on the bench. He sat down, sipped on his drink, and took a moment. He could hardly believe that he had just made his childhood dreams a reality.

5

FIGHT
FOR THE
FA CUP

After Marcus' dream start to life as a
professional soccer player, he became
a regular member of the first team.
Manchester United had not enjoyed a
top Premier League season. But they

were still in the FA Cup and had a good chance at progressing through the tournament.

Marcus joined the fun in the sixth round of the competition – a replay against West Ham United. The match was level until the 54th minute. The ball was played to Rashford on the edge of the penalty area. He skilfully carved his way through a handful of defenders before curling the ball with power and precision. It fired into the top right-hand corner. *Goal!* Marcus and United held on to the lead and set up a semi-final against Everton.

The semi-final was a difficult tie, but Manchester United emerged as victors. Marcus was going to get a chance to play in an FA Cup final, and potentially win a trophy in his first season as a professional soccer player.

On the 16th of May 2016, Wembley stadium was an incredible sight. Tens of thousands of fans poured into London with hopes of seeing their soccer heroes hold the prestigious FA Cup trophy. To the surprise of many, Crystal Palace were Manchester United's opponents. They had made it to the final for the second time in their history and were close to their dream of winning.

Manchester United, one of the most decorated clubs in English soccer, had won the FA Cup twelve times before. But since the end of Sir Alex Ferguson's time as manager, the club's trophy cabinet had not seen a new trophy for quite some time. The Premier League season was not going to plan as shock leaders Leicester City were running away with the league. So Manchester United looked at finding success in a domestic cup instead. Could Marcus and his teammates send thousands of fans into celebration? Or would he be heading home from his first final with a runner-up medal?

As Marcus and his teammates emerged from the Wembley tunnel, they were greeted by an atmosphere of excitement, tension and hope. Half of the stadium was filled with the blue and pink of Crystal Palace. The other half was a sea of Manchester United's red and white.

The referee blew the whistle, and the FA Cup final kicked off.

Crystal Palace scored first through Connor Wickham. However, the referee had already blown for a foul before the ball hit the net. So the game was pulled back to a free kick. United hit back with a chance of their own. Marcus glanced up from a run and spotted his teammate Marouane Fellaini. He delicately flicked the ball to Fellaini who struck a thunderous shot at goal. The ball cannoned off the post and left Fellaini tugging at his afro in frustration.

The first half remained goalless, as did most of the second half. Marcus had been playing well, and as the clock approached the 70th minute, he darted across the front of the Crystal Palace penalty box. Wilfried Zaha went shoulder to shoulder with Marcus and sent him tumbling to the ground. As Marcus lay there, disaster struck. Another Crystal Palace player, Yohan Cabaye, fell off balance and planted his foot on top of Marcus' knee. Marcus cried out in anguish as the studs bashed his knee. Marcus stayed on the ground and the medical staff came onto the field to assist him. But the pain was too great.

He couldn't continue playing. Marcus had been a shining light for the team and this was a hammer blow. Marcus sat on the bench with an ice pack tightly wrapped around his knee, and his fingers crossed that his teammates could get the job done.

Less than five minutes after Marcus' departure, the ball fell to Crystal Palace winger Jason Puncheon. He rifled the ball from the left-hand side of the penalty area. He struck the ball so hard that the United keeper, David De Gea, had little chance of stopping it. The Crystal Palace fans in the stadium erupted with delight, while Marcus and the Manchester United fans brought their hands to their heads. But before long, Marcus was shouting words of encouragement.

"There's still ten minutes. Let's make them count!" he shouted. His friend and teammate Jesse Lingard, within earshot, looked over to Marcus and nodded.

United did not let the setback ruin the game. The club's captain, Wayne Rooney, sprinted across the field past the Crystal Palace midfield and defense. He sent over a cross and

Fellaini brought the ball down with his chest. The speedy Spanish winger Juan Mata met the ball on the volley with his left foot and equalized. Marcus and the other players on the bench celebrated. United hadn't been behind for long, and they were still in this tie.

Neither team was able to score a winner by the 90th minute, so extra time was needed. Things got harder for United during extra time as their center back, Chris Smalling, was sent off after getting a second yellow card. If United were going to do this, they were going to have to do it with one less man than the opposition. Added to this, their talented forward Marcus was on the bench! But United gave it everything they had. Even with one less player, they still appeared dangerous. Their right back, Antonio Valencia, swung in a cross. It was stolen by a defender but bounced out to the edge of the penalty area.

Jesse Lingard met the ball with his right foot. He sent an unstoppable volley into the net. *Winning goal!* It sent the Manchester United fans in the stadium, and at home watching on TV, into a frenzy.

The team held on in the remaining minutes. As the final whistle blew, Marcus, who was still in pain, jogged onto the field and celebrated with his teammates. It was as if the pain wasn't there. The only thing Marcus could think about was that he was now part of a team that had won the FA Cup. In his first season as a professional soccer player, he had played a part in winning a trophy for his boyhood team.

6

NATIONAL TEAM DREAMS

As the 2015/2016 Premier League season neared its end, Marcus kept training to the best of his ability. He picked up the ball at the edge of the box and darted around fellow

teammate Phil Jones, sending him tumbling to the floor. He neatly placed a curler into the top corner.

"That's a wrap," said the coach, with a grin.

"Give us a hand, Rashy," said Jones.

Marcus reached out and helped his teammate to his feet.

"How do you feel?" said Jones.

"I feel fine," said Marcus, not quite sure what Jones was getting at.

"Fine!" said Jones. "I'd be doing cartwheels if I were you, lad."

"What are you on about?" said Marcus as they walked together.

"The England squad. You've been picked," said Jones.

"Very funny," laughed Marcus.

Jones scratched his head and quickly turned around to their teammates.

"He doesn't know!" said Jones.

"You have been selected," said the coach. "You're going to France."

Believing he was being pranked, Marcus walked into the changing room. As if he'd be going to the Euros! He'd only made his pro debut a couple of months ago. Why would he be called up for England? Marcus took his phone from his locker. It was pinging

with messages. He saw ones from his
mom, his brothers and his friends.

"England!!!!!" one of them read.

"I'm so proud of you!" read another.

He sat down. He couldn't think,
speak or even move.

Marcus brought his hands to his
eyes and rubbed them—he couldn't
believe what he was seeing, and
he held back tears. A smile burst
from him. He brought up the squad
announcement on his
phone and he was there.
The forwards read:
Wayne Rooney, Harry

Kane, Jamie Vardy, Daniel Sturridge and ... Marcus Rashford.

He hadn't just been called up to play for England. Marcus was going to play in one of the biggest competitions in international soccer!

As a disappointing Premier League season for United came to a close, Marcus joined the national team. Before flying to France for the major competition, there was a warm-up match to contend with. Marcus got a chance to wear the three lions shirt for the first time in a friendly against Australia.

The Stadium of Light was filled with fans excited for the upcoming tournament. Yet before some fans had even taken their seat, they missed something incredible. In the 3rd minute of the match, Raheem Sterling dinked the ball into the penalty area. The ball deflected into the air off an Australian defender and Marcus met the ball on the volley. *Goal!* The ball struck the netting making him, at 18-years-old, the youngest ever English player to score on his debut. Marcus had now scored on his Europa League, his Premier League *and* his

international debut. England won the tie 2-1 and headed to the tournament in France with high spirits. All across England, fans crossed their fingers for success at a major international competition.

However, things did not go to plan for Roy Hodgson's England. In the first knockout round, the team met a surprise in a tie against Iceland. It was a game where England were heavy favorites to progress to the next round. Yet they were eliminated by the underdogs and sent home from the tournament embarrassed and defeated.

Marcus enjoyed his time with the team, but only featured for a handful of minutes during the tournament. Still, he cherished each one and could hardly believe that he played for England.

Following the shock loss, Roy Hodgson resigned. He would no longer manage the England team. Change was happening in the England camp. And as Marcus returned to Manchester United, changes were happening there too. After a poor Premier League season, Louis Van Gaal had been removed as manager. In his place, to the surprise of many, an experienced and celebrated soccer manager arrived. He was a character, a winner and a manager not to get on the wrong side of. In the upcoming season, Marcus was going to be managed by José Mourinho.

7
THE SPECIAL ONE

In preparation for the 2016/2017 Premier League campaign, Marcus returned to Old Trafford for pre-season training. As soon as he walked through the training ground door, he was asked to go and meet the new manager.

The old plaque on the office door had been replaced with a shiny new golden one.

José Mourinho.

Marcus knocked on the door and took a step back. This was a manager who had won the Premier League, Champions League and plenty of cups. Marcus couldn't help but feel nervous. He straightened his back as the door opened.

"Marcus!" said Mourinho. "Come and take a seat."

Mourinho sat behind his desk and Marcus sat in a chair opposite.

Marcus looked around the room. It had changed completely since the last time he had sat there with Van Gaal. Now there was a tactics board stuck to the wall, managerial awards lining the desk and the pictures scattered across the walls showed Mourinho's victories as a coach. But the biggest change of them all was the new manager sitting across the desk looking directly at him.

"It is an honor to meet you," said Mourinho.

"Likewise," said Marcus.

"If you'd played the full ninety minutes against Iceland, I think you'd have won," Mourinho grinned.

Marcus laughed. "If you say so."

"Anyway—brand new season," said Mourinho, rubbing his hands together. "A new manager is a blank canvas."

"I like the sound of that," said Marcus.

"I'm very excited to manage you. You have incredible talent. I know you are a winner just like me. Trust me, we're going to do something. They do not call me The Special One for no reason!"

Mourinho helped Marcus develop as a soccer player, teaching him that he didn't need to score goal after goal to win.

A 1-0 victory was just as important as a 6-4 victory. To Mourinho soccer was about winning at all costs. The new manager also instilled a mental toughness in Marcus. When Marcus first started as a professional soccer player, everything had gone to plan. He'd scored on his debuts and wowed the world. But after his England trip, he had to deal with adversity for the first time. Being a soccer player wasn't always about the highs, but about how he could develop and improve during the lows.

Marcus found his first year playing with Mourinho difficult. While Mourinho helped him to grow as a player, Marcus' individual numbers for the team had taken a hit. He made thirty-two appearances for Manchester United in the Premier League, but only scored five goals and provided two assists. This was impressive for a young player enjoying his first full Premier League season, but after Marcus' blistering start, he had been hoping for more. And Mourinho still believed that he was a winner.

Despite another mediocre Premier League season, the club had won silverware in a Community Shield victory against Leicester City, and a League Cup win against Southampton. Marcus and Manchester United had a chance to turn a disappointing season into a good one as they battled their way to the final of the Europa League.

Standing in their way were Ajax, a formidable Eredivisie side from the Netherlands. In order to claim the Europa League trophy and save their season, Manchester United needed to win. Were they up to the task?

8

EUROPA LEAGUE BATTLE

The Friends Arena in Stockholm, Sweden was packed. On a warm spring evening fans had traveled to watch Manchester United vs Ajax. The Red Devils needed a win

to improve on a poor season. Ajax, meanwhile, aimed for victory in their first major European final since 1996.

Marcus led the line for United and came onto the field ready to perform. But standing in his way was the young and hungry Ajax team, who hoped to upset the odds.

Manchester United struck first with a deflected strike in the 17th minute. The club's record £89 million signing Paul Pogba struck from outside of the box. His shot hit a defender before looping past the keeper. Marcus joined his teammate in celebration,

but there was still plenty of soccer to be played.

After the goal, Ajax dominated possession and had chance after chance. Yet they could not break the United defense. Marcus and his teammates caught their breath with a 48th minute corner. The ball was swung into the box and Marcus made a run to distract the defense. Chris Smalling got his head to the ball. He prodded it toward the goal. Manchester United midfielder Henrikh Mkhitaryan, reacting quicker than any of the defenders, leaned back and flicked the ball into the net. *Goal!* The away fans went wild.

 Marcus and his teammates held on to the lead and won the Europa League. This was the only major European trophy Manchester United had left to win. Now they joined the likes of Ajax, Chelsea, Juventus and Bayern Munich in having won every single one.

Marcus, Mourinho and Manchester United carried their strong performance into the following 2017/2018 Premier League season. They claimed a second-place finish behind rivals Manchester City. This was their best finish since the departure of Sir Alex Ferguson in 2013. While it did hurt to lose to their Manchester rivals, United's rise from sixth place in 2017 to second place in 2018 was to be admired. It was a sign that, under Mourinho, Manchester United were moving in a positive direction. Marcus made thirty-five appearances for the club during the Premier League season. He improved on his previous year's tally with seven goals and five assists.

Yet, as the Premier League season ended, Marcus was not lying on a sun lounger on faraway shores. With two years having passed since the 2016 Euros, it was time for the 2018 World Cup in Russia. England had a new manager, Gareth Southgate. But this had not changed Marcus' position in the squad. No matter who was in charge, there was no question about Marcus' ability. He was one of the best young English players. And so, Southgate picked Marcus as a member of the 2018 World Cup squad. Would soccer be coming home this time?

9

WORLD CUP 2018

Marcus arrived in Russia with the England Squad in high spirits. Despite his young age, to some he was considered an experienced player, having played in a major tournament before. Yet this was still his first World Cup.

Playing for Manchester United, with so much pressure and expectation, had prepared Marcus for the highs, lows and constant pressure that follow the English national team. This wasn't a stage where Marcus would hide, but one where he hoped to stand out.

Much like Marcus' previous national team experience, England got through the group stages. England snuck a last-minute winner against Tunisia in their first game, demolished new-boys Panama in their second, but were defeated by Belgium in their third. However, they still progressed from their group as runners up.

Instead of warming the bench as he did in the previous tournament, Marcus got the chance to play. He took the full ninety minutes against Belgium and had an appearance off the bench against Tunisia.

In the 16-16 tie, England were drawn against Colombia. It was at this hurdle that England and Marcus had previously fallen. It was something that neither Marcus nor team and country wanted to experience again. The South American side were fierce and strong; well known for their enthusiasm and grit.

Both sides were alert and did not allow any goals in the first half. England went into the lead via a penalty in the 57th minute. Harry Kane was dragged to the ground during a corner by a Colombian defender and was awarded a penalty. The top scorer of the tournament, Kane easily scored the penalty and England looked like they were headed toward the quarterfinals. But Colombia still had something to say about that.

In injury time, as the final seconds of the match were being played,

Colombia had a corner. They sent every player up toward goal, including their goalkeeper, and the ball was swung into the box. The towering defender Yerry Mina met the ball with a thunderous header. England's Jordan Pickford could only grasp at thin air as the net rippled behind him. The Colombian team ran to their fans and celebrated as the England team fell to the ground dejected. The score was level and they were heading to extra time.

Neither team could find a winner during the additional period. Marcus

was brought onto the field to try and force a goal in the dying minutes. But even with Marcus on the field, England could not find a winner. At yet another major soccer tournament, the match was going to be decided in a fashion that sends chills down the spine of any English fan.

Penalties.

Never before had England won a penalty shoot-out in a World Cup.

Was defeat inevitable?

Colombia took the first spot kick. Radamel Falcao, an experienced striker, coolly struck the ball into the middle of the goal making the score 1-0. England's captain Kane responded instantly by scoring his spot kick and leveling it to 1-1. Colombia regained their lead with a fine strike by Juan Cuadradro. His strike found the top left-hand corner. England's next taker was Marcus. He was a fine finisher and a strong penalty taker. Yet during a pressured situation, sometimes it doesn't matter how good you are. It's all about whether you can handle your nerves.

Marcus was thrown the ball by his goalkeeper.

"Come on Rashy, you've got this!" said Pickford.

Marcus placed the ball onto the spot. He stepped back, tuning out the jeers and chants from the Colombian supporters. He focused solely on where he was going to place his penalty. He sidestepped to the left, slowed his run and made his way to the ball. He struck it and … scored! It was 2-2.

Luis Muriel took Colombia's third penalty and found the net. It was 3-2 Colombia.

Jordan Henderson stepped up next, juggling the ball on the edge of the box before his kick. He struck the ball to the right but the Colombian goalkeeper, David Ospina, dived and met it with his hand. England had missed and Colombia had the advantage. Mateus Uribe stepped up for Colombia. If he scored they would have a two goal advantage. Pickford needed to make the save to keep England's dream alive. Uribe ran up to the ball and thumped it .... but it hit the crossbar and bounced out! England still had a chance.

Kieran Tripper was up next for England, and he calmly scored his penalty. It was 3-3. Carlos Bacca, a Colombian substitute, took the next penalty. Yet Pickford, leaping into the air with cat-like reflexes, was able to stop it. To progress to the next round and emerge with their first World Cup penalty shoot-out victory, England needed just one more goal. Marcus stood with his teammates on the halfway line as Eric Dier strolled up to the ball. He stood behind it, arms tucked in tightly to his sides. As he stood there, thousands of fans edged further along their seats. Finally, Dier ran up to the ball and banished England's penalty demons. *He scored!* Marcus and his teammates ran to congratulate him. They'd done it. They'd won a penalty shoot-out and had made it to a World Cup quarterfinal.

England went on to defeat Sweden 0-2 in the quarterfinal, before falling to Croatia 2-1 in the semifinal. Despite not winning the tournament, Marcus and his teammates returned home as heroes.

10
SOLSKJÆR'S RETURN

While Marcus had experienced delight away with England, the same could not be said for his return to Manchester United. The Red Devils started the 2018/2019 Premier League season poorly. They had early defeats to Brighton, Tottenham, West

Ham, Manchester City and Liverpool. The club were also embarrassingly knocked out of the League Cup in a penalty shoot-out loss to Derby County. With the club having made big investments during Mourinho's reign, these results weren't good enough. During a cold and gloomy winter, José Mourinho was sacked as Manchester United manager.

In an attempt to lift morale, Manchester United brought in a familiar face to manage the team on a temporary basis.

A former Manchester United legend, nicknamed the baby-faced assassin: Ole Gunnar Solskjær.

As the new manager walked onto the training ground, all of the players gathered. A glimpse of the sun peaked out from behind the clouds.

"Well, it's been a whirlwind few days," said Solskjær. "I'm delighted to be back. I feel like I'm home."

Marcus, who had been taking part in shooting drills, sat down to catch his breath.

"Look, you've got me for six months. Let's see what we can do together," said Solskjær, a great smile beaming from him. Some of the overseas players leaned in closer as they tried to understand his Norweigan-Mancunian accent.

"This club is something else," said Solskjær. "Look around. This is Manchester United, the biggest soccer club in the world. I want smiles, happy faces, commitment. Never forget how amazing it is to be here. Because soon you'll be old and gray like me! Now then, let's play some soccer."

The return of Solskjær brought an effortless energy and positivity to the club. It was a feeling that had been missing for quite some time. The caretaker manager had an instant impact. Under his stewardship Manchester United regained fine form before faltering slightly at the end of the season. Solskjær's appointment worked wonders for Marcus. Having a former striker as a manager was a way for him to learn from one of the greats. Despite a difficult start to the season, Marcus achieved fantastic personal numbers.

He had ten goals and seven assists in the Premier League.

Having impressed everybody, Solskjær's temporary contract was turned into a permanent one. In the spring of 2019, Ole Gunnar Solskjær became the official manager of Manchester United.

11

MARCUS RASHFORD MBE

The 2019/2020 Premier League season was like no other. Marcus, Solskjær and Manchester United enjoyed a reasonably successful season together. Marcus achieved

his best scoring tally of seventeen goals and nine assists. However, 2020 was a year where soccer took a back seat. It was the year COVID-19 became a global pandemic. As the UK underwent lockdown, chanting crowds and full stands became empty stadiums overnight. Soccer matches stopped. Life was put on hold and schools were closed to all but a few children.

Having relied so heavily on free school meals during his youth, Marcus was worried about children going hungry during the pandemic.

He understood just how much those free meals meant to the children. The moment school doors were closed, Marcus started working with a food charity to help provide for those vulnerable children. With Marcus' help, the charity was able to raise £20 million to provide meals for 3 million people.

Marcus was at home after a workout session one evening, feeling exhausted. For a minute or two he just wanted to sit down on the sofa and watch TV. He rested his sore legs on the sofa's arm and leaned back into a cushion.

"Breaking news," said the

newsreader, shuffling her documents. "The government has decided not to extend the free school meal vouchers scheme for children over the summer holidays."

Marcus dropped the remote on the floor.

"I can't believe it," he said, shocked.

Marcus reached for his phone.

"Mom!" said Marcus.

"What is it?" his mom answered. "You sound really upset."

"Have you seen the news?" he said. "They're canceling free school meal vouchers."

"That's terrible!" said his mom. "Those poor kids need them."

"Just like we did," said Marcus, pacing around his living room. "I've got to do something,"

"Then do it," said his mom. "Use your platform for good."

With help from his personal team, Marcus drafted a letter to the government. He shared it on Twitter, pleading for the extension of free school meal vouchers for children. Within hours the tweet went viral, with hundreds of thousands of likes and media coverage on most

TV channels. Marcus had brought this issue to attention and now the pressure was falling on the government to answer. The day after Marcus' letter was posted online, while chatting with his family at home, Marcus felt his phone vibrating in his pocket. He left the room and stood outside.

"Hello?" said Marcus.

"Hello, Marcus. This is the Prime Minister, Boris Johnson," said the voice at the other end.

Marcus was taken aback. "Evening ... Prime Minister."

"Sorry to bother you at this time," said Mr. Johnson. "Let me get to the point of why I'm disturbing your peace and quiet. I wanted to let you know, personally, that your efforts and voice have been heard. We will be providing a COVID summer food fund. It will make sure 1.3 million children do not go without meals."

"That's amazing!" said Marcus. "Thank you, Prime Minister. But this can't be the end of it. There's more to do to make sure children don't go hungry."

It was another moment of great success off the field, not just for

Marcus but for so many families across the country. And it did indeed turn out that there was plenty more to do.

After the school summer break, it was announced that the government was not continuing the free school meal vouchers. Again, Marcus led a long campaign over many months. He was supported by many businesses and organizations who joined him to help out in their local communities. Finally, the government announced a winter fund, providing free meals until the following spring. Marcus was with his family in the kitchen when he received the phone call confirming it. As he told them all the news, the room was lit up with smiles, relieved laughter and one or two tears.

Marcus earned many awards for his efforts off the field in 2020. While training with the England squad for a Nations League match against Belgium, Marcus received the news that he had been named on the Queen's birthday list of honors. He had been awarded a special title because of his work toward helping vulnerable children during the COVID-19 pandemic. At the age of

22, Marcus wasn't only a top player for Manchester United and a goal scorer for his national team. He was also an honored MBE recipient and voice for a community that needed help.

Marcus had not done all of this on his own. While he had worked hard with his close team to realize this goal, there was one individual who had played a bigger part than most. Marcus' mother had done so much for him and his siblings. While Marcus got awards left, right and center, he wanted to make sure that his mother received the recognition that she deserved.

A day after the call, Marcus and his mom visited a new food depot that had been created to help provide food for vulnerable families.

"That high-vis vest suits you," joked Marcus' mom.

"Thanks, I guess," said Marcus.

The pair of them followed a couple of volunteers who were walking across the depot with a handful of others.

"We're just approaching our new building," said the volunteer. "And, if you wouldn't mind, we'd like to name it after your mom."

Marcus and his mom stood in front of the building with his mom proudly holding a golden plaque aloft: *Melanie Maynard House.*

The pair of them smiled for photos not too many miles away from where they'd experienced their struggles as a family. Years ago, they had relied on places such as these to feed their family, and now they were giving back to a cause that meant the world to them.

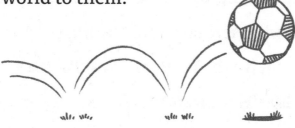

EURO 2020

Marcus was selected for the England squad for the European Football Championship 2020. England were battling against twenty-four teams for the right to be crowned as champions. But first there were friendlies to play. In the final preparation match for the tournament, England faced

Romania at the Riverside Stadium in Middlesborough. For Marcus, this wasn't just a friendly, but a match that he would remember forever. In recognition of his team spirit, as well as his leadership, Gareth Southgate named Marcus as captain for the match.

Marcus led the team out of the Wembley tunnel with the captain's armband tightly wrapped around his arm. To top off a great day, Marcus

 scored the only goal of the match—he tucked away a penalty and celebrated with the fans. England were heading into the tournament off the back of a win, and with a wave of excitement.

Was this going to be England's year?

England had been placed in Group D. To progress to the knockout rounds of the tournament, they needed to perform against Croatia, Scotland and Czech Republic.

Euro 2020 matches took place across eleven countries. Marcus and England played their first three games at Wembley. With home support and a team stacked with talented players, the time for just dreaming was over. England were able to progress from their group at the top of the table, having defeated Croatia and Czech Republic, and drawn against a stubborn Scottish side. It set up a mouthwatering tie against Germany in the round of 16.

England and Germany have always had a fierce rivalry, with Germany often coming out on top. But with this England squad, a win felt possible. A big part of that feeling was team unity. Although Marcus had only played a handful of minutes in the tournament, he was part of a supportive squad. No matter the outcome or teamsheet, the players put their country above their personal feelings.

In this ferocious tie, the deadlock wasn't broken until the 75th minute. Sterling scored following a Luke Shaw cross. Then, only minutes later, Sterling almost undid his hard work. He lost the ball and the German team pounced on the counterattack. Thomas Müller ran through on goal and shot, but he fired wide. An entire nation sighed in relief. In the

86th minute, Kane got his first goal of the tournament, which cemented England's victory.

England then defeated Ukraine in the quarterfinal and needed extra time to get past a difficult Denmark team. With a massive effort, England found themselves in their first ever Euros final. It was the first time England had made it to the final of a major international tournament since 1966! Could England end their 55-year wait for a trophy? There was one more country they needed to overcome ...

Italy—a team unbeaten in thirty-three games.

In front of a roaring Wembley crowd, England got off to the perfect start. Inside of three minutes, Shaw found the back of the net following a Trippier cross, sending England fans in the stadium, and across the country, wild. But Italy did not let this early goal upset their rhythm, and they fought back. For an hour, the English defense stood strong. However, their defense was finally broken in the 67th minute. After a scramble in the box following a corner, Leonardo Bonucci prodded home an equalizer. Both sides were unable to score a winner within ninety minutes, or even in extra time. This final was to be settled by penalties. But before the referee blew his final whistle, Gareth Southgate wanted to make a substitution.

"I believe in you, Marcus," said Southgate.

Marcus and Jadon Sancho were brought on to take part in a crucial round of penalties. England were only a handful of spot kicks away from Euro 2020 glory. Marcus stepped up as

England's third penalty taker. England had the advantage, with Pickford having saved Andrea Belotti's penalty.

The shootout score was 2-2. Marcus needed to score to keep the advantage. This was his chance to shine. He took a slow run up, waiting carefully to see where the goalkeeper was going. The goalkeeper moved first and dived to his right. Marcus shot to the left. But he had gone too far! The ball clipped the post. Marcus had missed. The strength left his legs, and he bent over in disbelief, his head in his hands. He returned to his teammates with his head down, unable to speak. They refused to let him suffer.

"Head up," they told him. "It's not over yet."

Standing shoulder to shoulder, they watched the rest of the penalty shootout unfold together.

After Marcus' miss, the tide had turned. He was not the only English player to miss their spot kick. Jadon Sancho and Bukayo Saka also missed their penalties. Italy were crowned as European champions. As the last penalty hit the gloves of Player of the Tournament, Italian goalkeeper

Gianluigi Donnarumma, the Italian players sprinted to their hero and celebrated. The English players sunk to their knees and held their hands over their eyes. They were so close, but yet so far. Southgate came onto the field to meet his players. He made sure to come over to Marcus. This was a feeling that the manager knew well. In the 1996 Euros, Southgate had missed the deciding penalty of a semifinal for England.

"I'm so proud of you," said Southgate.

Marcus had no words. Southgate put his arm around him.

"You're more than just one kick. This night won't define you."

"I've let everyone down," said Marcus, sadly.

"You haven't. It takes so much courage to step up to take a penalty. Even the best players miss. You've played your part in bringing your country to the final of the Euros. England has never got this far before. You're a historymaker."

Marcus looked up to the fans. Thousands of them were applauding their team. A mixture of pride and sadness filled the stadium.

"You're more than a soccer player," Southgate continued. "You've done so much, not just in soccer but through your work outside of it. Remember that. It's okay to feel all of this, but don't forget just how remarkable all your work has been. You've got so much more ahead of you."

Gareth left to talk to the other players. Marcus stood still and looked across the stadium. This England team had given everything. He was part of a side that had brought so much joy and hope to an entire nation. They had shown just how talented and capable they were. They had shown that with a young team—with star players like Marcus Rashford—anything was possible. It might not have come home in Euro 2020. But there was a strong sense of hope that soccer would come home in the years to come.

13
ROAD TO
QATAR 2022

After an incredible tournament with
England, it was time for Marcus
to finally relax. It was a chance to
take a short break from soccer and
reflect on the wild events of the past
couple of years. Marcus made time
for everything he cared most about:

spending time with his friends, family and providing help for people who needed it. While soccer had always been his life, he'd started something far bigger off the field. He was the champion for a national movement to make sure that children never went hungry.

Marcus decided to make a surprise appearance and help out at a local food bank. As he stepped into the food bank, the volunteers froze on the spot. They burst into applause and thanked him for all that he'd done. Marcus quickly asked for them to stop.

"Thank you," he said. "But you're the real heroes."

At the back of the food bank, there was a small playground where children were running around. Some were kicking a soccer, while the others were chatting and laughing with their friends. Here, kids didn't need to worry about rumbling tummies or empty plates. They could just focus on enjoying themselves.

Like the volunteers, the children's eyes widened as they realized who had just arrived. One fearless boy ran up to Marcus and pointed at him.

"Rashford!" he said, open-mouthed.

"Hello, little man," said Marcus. "What are you up to?"

"Playing!" he said. "Do you want to play?"

"Go on then," smiled Marcus.

Another boy gathered himself after the surprise of seeing the Manchester United player. "Please can we have an autograph?"

"Of course," said Marcus. "You can all have pictures, too, if you want."

Smiles burst from all of their faces. Marcus had once been the little boy waiting

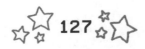

at a food bank. No matter how rich or how famous he'd become, he'd always make sure to give back to his community. He would be a supportive figure for those who needed help, just as he had needed it once.